Highlights

More Hidden Pictures Puzzles to Highlight

HIGHLIGHTS PRESS

Honesdale, Pennsylvania

hot dog

paintbrush

toothbrush

crescent moon

spoon

leaf

slice of pizza

pickle

fried egg

ice-cream cone

banana

hat

3

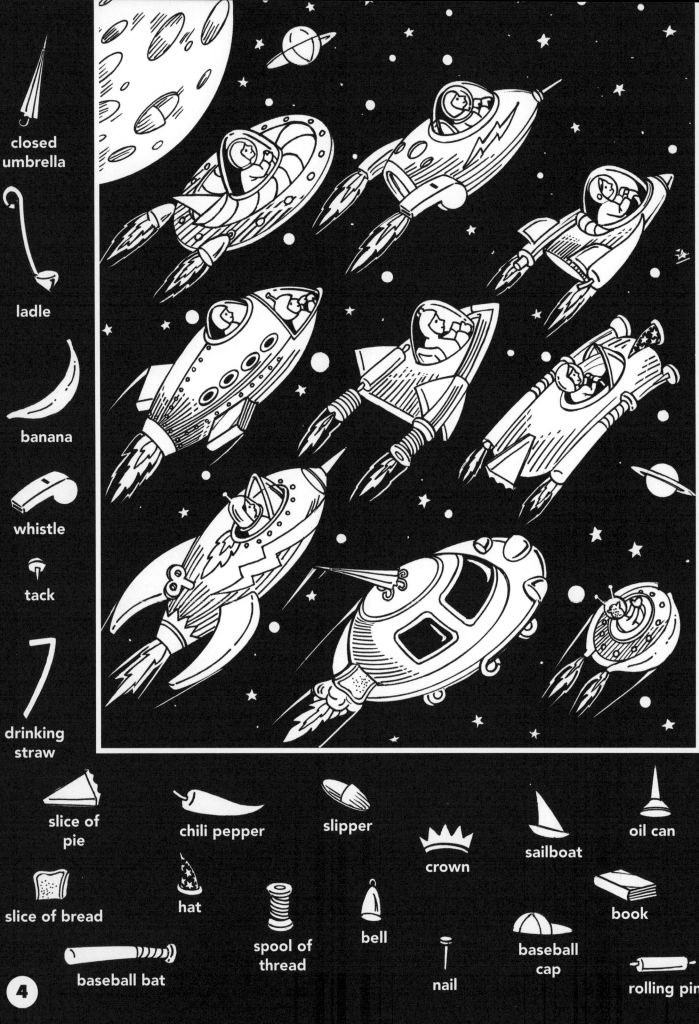

closed umbrella

ladle

banana

whistle

tack

drinking straw

slice of pie

chili pepper

slipper

crown

sailboat

oil can

slice of bread

hat

spool of thread

bell

book

baseball bat

nail

baseball cap

rolling pin

mitten

mushroom

artist's brush

fish

paper clip

banana

saw

teacup

ice-cream cone

heart

toothbrush

5

fish

kite

elf's hat

wedge of cheese

pencil

horn

bell

crescent moon

candy cane

toothbrush

sock

carrot

7

mop

ladle

glove

needle

spoon

ring

heart

slice of
watermelon

artist's
brush

musical
note

candle

screw

mallet

spoon

crescent moon

artist's brush

necktie

stethoscope

belt

boomerang

yo-yo

slice of pie

banana

pencil

boot

chili pepper

mug

necktie

sock

chili pepper

piece of popcorn

heart

wedge of lemon

olive

button

pear

slice of pizza

sneaker

shuttlecock

bobby pin

comb

needle

butterfly

butter knife

mushroom

cupcake

paper clip

crown

crescent moon

fish

whistle

test tube

snake

comb

flute

artist's
brush

fish

spoon

fried egg

wishbone

hammer

baseball
bat

mushroom

closed
umbrella

stool

magic wand

glove

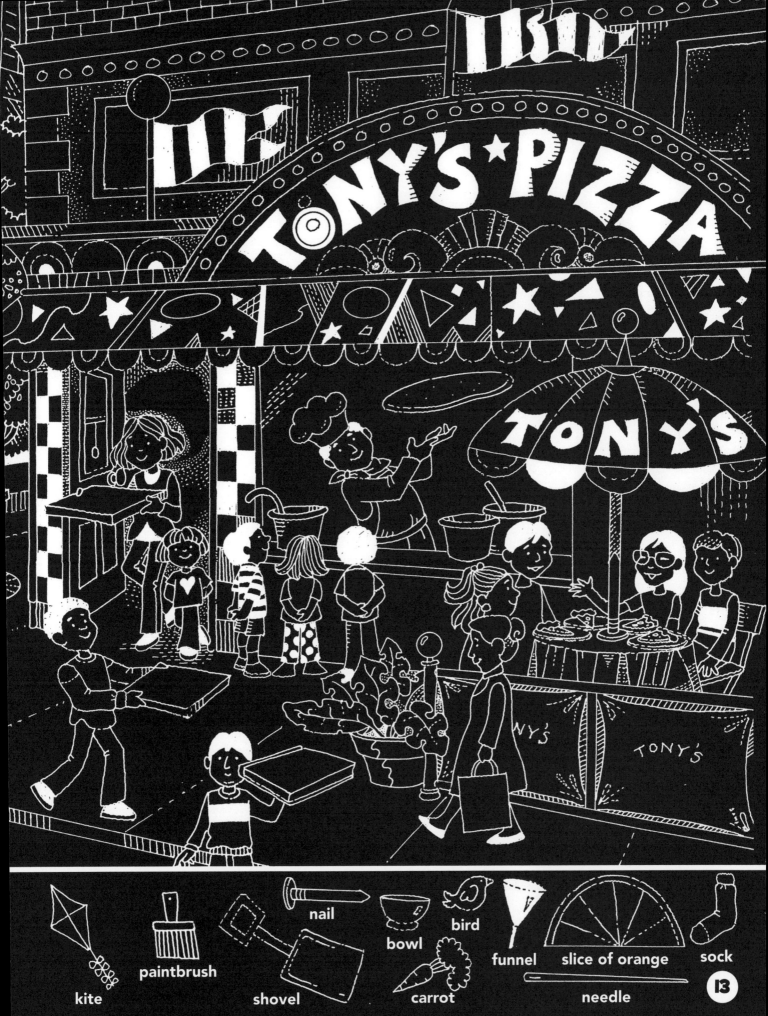

kite paintbrush shovel nail bowl bird carrot funnel slice of orange needle sock

cupcake

hockey stick

crown

lollipop

ice-cream cone

toothbrush

hammer

rolling pin

snake

cotton swab

shuttlecock

comb

envelope

bell

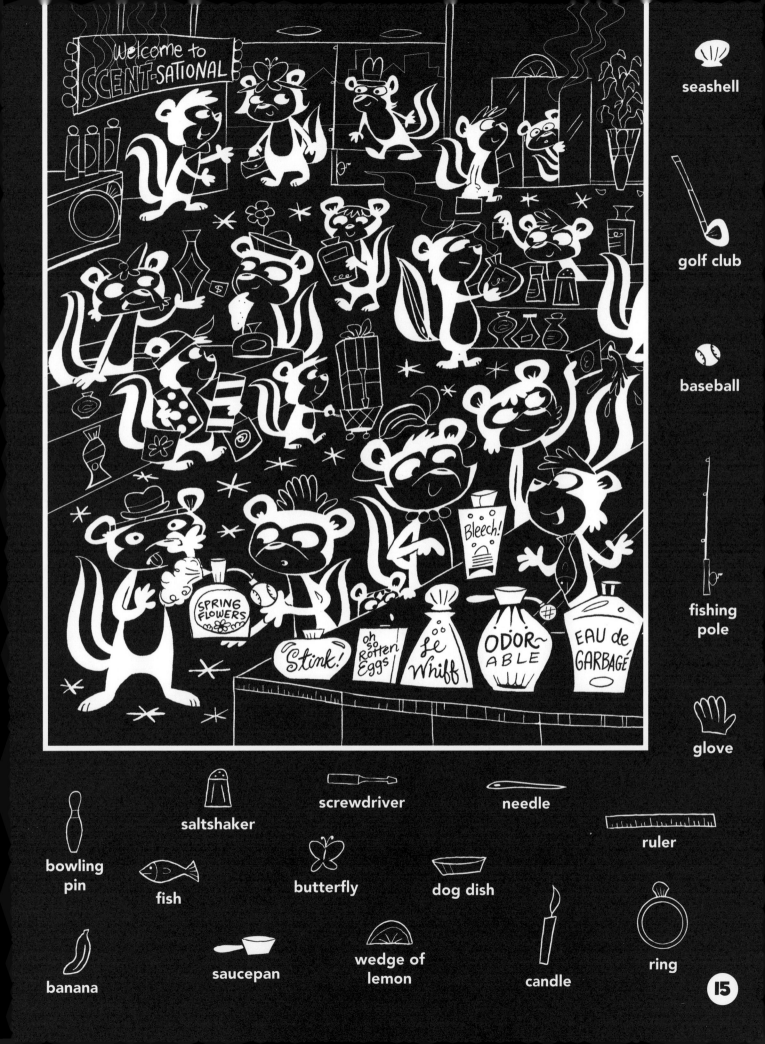

seashell

golf club

baseball

fishing pole

glove

saltshaker

screwdriver

needle

ruler

bowling pin

fish

butterfly

dog dish

banana

saucepan

wedge of lemon

candle

ring

cane

sheep

acorn

saltshaker

spoon

kite

crescent moon

slice of pie

heart

toothbrush

carrot

envelope

pencil

mug

book

sailboat

plate

pointy hat

bow tie

fish

spoon

artist's brush

ring

needle

hockey stick

frog

nail

closed umbrella

arrow

sailboat

fish

ice-cream cone

hockey
stick

light bulb

drinking
straw

teacup

nail

sock

slice of
pie

banana

crescent
moon

cherries

coat hanger

snake

pencil

fish

needle

toothbrush

comb

sailboat

top hat

18

crown

pencil

bell

teacup

snake

baseball bat

glove

envelope

boomerang

carrot

pear

heart

19

teacup   lighthouse   umbrella   glove   domino   popcorn
bowling pin   mitten   heart

20

crown

dog bone headphones fishhook feather duster slice of pizza mushroom lollipop fried egg scissors bacon

21

peanut

slice of
bread

teacup

pennant

banana

egg

apple

acorn

crown

open book

steering
wheel

olive

heart

high-heeled shoe

22

ball of yarn

snowcone

party hat

teacup

snowman

snake

adhesive bandage

crayon

fish

sock

toothbrush

pencil

wedge of lemon

ice-cream cone

slice of pizza

domino

23

comb

candy corn

slice of pizza

ruler

shuttlecock

lollipop

pitcher   bell   carrot   crescent moon   crown   mug

spatula

needle

snake

fish

dog bone

kite

chef's hat

fan

drinking straw

turtle

party hat

ladder

26

skateboard

gingerbread man

broccoli

green bean

muffin

spoon

heart

nail

eyeglasses

inchworm

fishhook

paper airplane

artist's brush

chili pepper

banana

heart

wishbone

teacup

pennant

gravy bowl

shoe

boomerang

bell

frying pan

building block

envelope

canoe

trowel

snail

paper clip

comb

crayon

hat

button

glove

fish

flyswatter

arrow

eyeglasses

lollipop

scissors

banana

broccoli

kite

flower

toothbrush

29

handbag

mushroom

flower pot

drum

key

peanut

fish

saw

belt

ladder carrot rolling pin tube of toothpaste flashlight toothbrush feather scissors crown ladle banana apple slice of pizza

kite

necktie

fishhook

teacup

coin

comb

surfboard

knitted hat

open book

paintbrush

microphone

top hat

magnifying glass

spider

slice of bacon

mushroom

pennant

flowerpot

log

slice of pizza

32

closed umbrella

sailboat

paper clip

dog

horn

pencil

crown

banana

wishbone

heart

toothbrush

bell

crescent moon

33

ladder

cane

bell

banana

candle

loaf of bread

pear

purse

feather

frying pan

tennis racket

arrow

hot dog

fried egg

carrot

boot

toothbrush

dog bone

envelope

screwdriver

belt

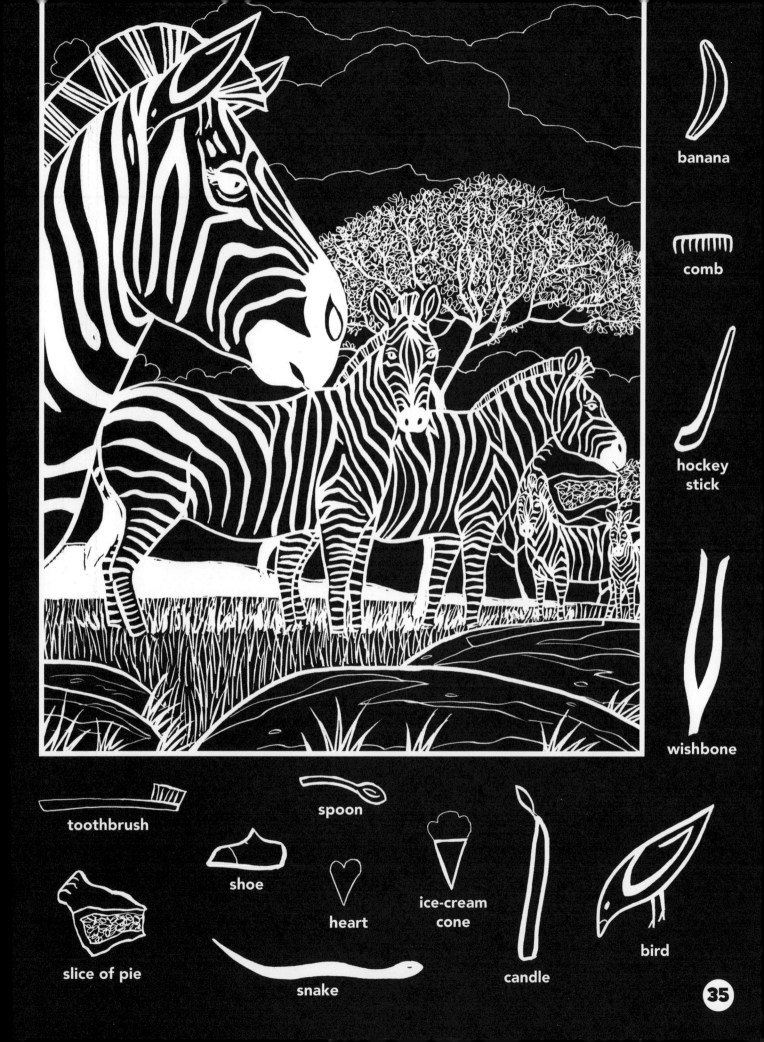

banana

comb

hockey stick

wishbone

toothbrush

spoon

shoe

heart

ice-cream cone

candle

bird

slice of pie

snake

35

golf club

needle

carrot

funnel

tack

teacup

open book

candle

baseball bat

toothbrush

pencil

banana

snake

nail

heart

ring

shovel

drinking straw

36

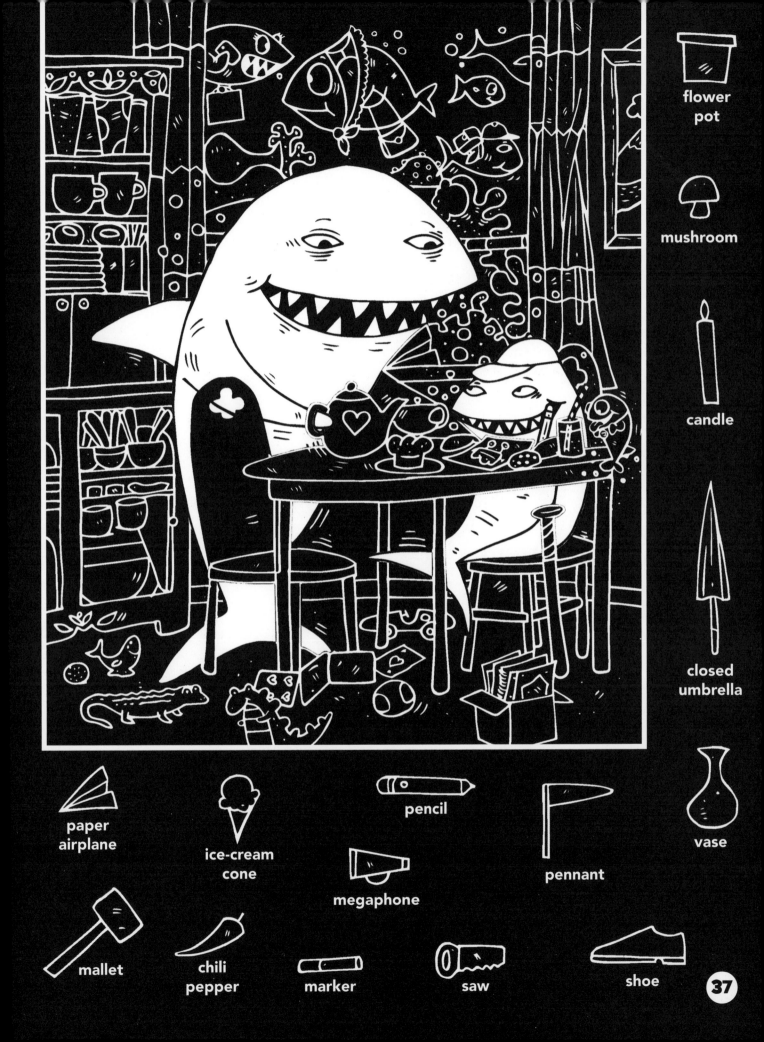

flower pot

mushroom

candle

closed umbrella

vase

paper airplane

ice-cream cone

pencil

megaphone

pennant

mallet

chili pepper

marker

saw

shoe

37

button
mitten
book
carrot
domino
basketball
cupcake
banana

pencil

ruler

wedge of
lemon

heart

pear

ring

crescent
moon

envelope

glove

39

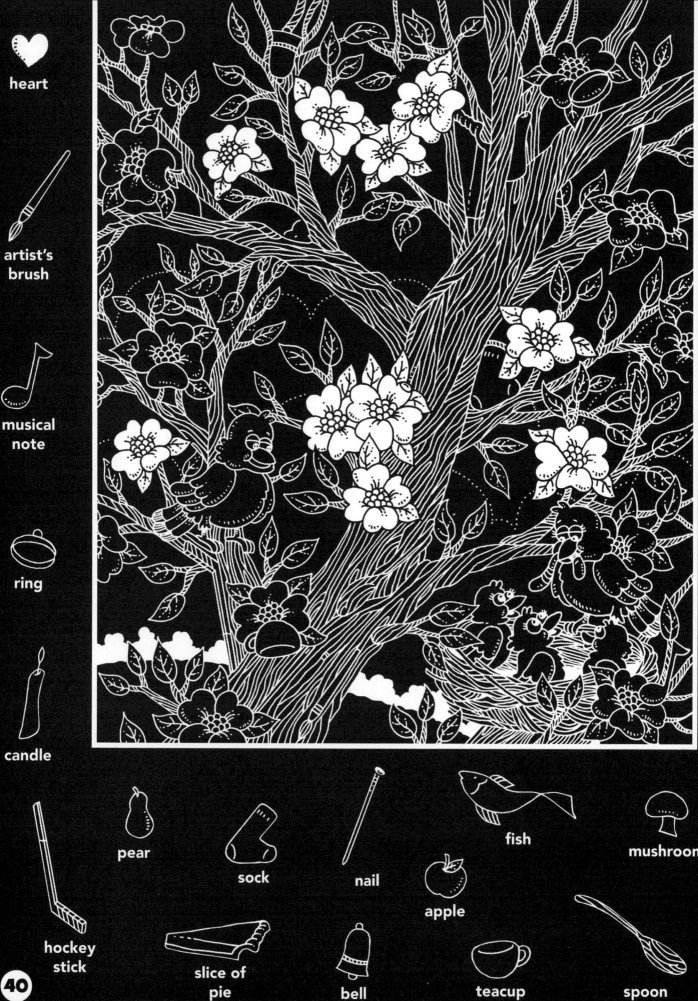

heart

artist's brush

musical note

ring

candle

pear

sock

nail

fish

mushroom

hockey stick

slice of pie

bell

apple

teacup

spoon

40

ring

paper clip

mallet

ice-cream cone

crescent moon

lock

bagel

slice of pizza

toothbrush

ice skate

sock

envelope

bell

slipper

MONSTER MASH

comb
flag
baseball
matchstick
candy corn
sailboat
safety pin
eyeglasses
ice-cream cone
domino
wedge of lemon
crescent moon
megaphone
slice of pizza
leaf
umbrella
ring

bowl

mushroom

hockey stick

envelope

traffic light

bell

ladle

artist's brush

banana

sock

tack

boomerang

drinking straw

fishhook

piece of popcorn

tube of toothpaste

carrot

43

hockey stick

lollipop

candy cane

ring

magnet

sock

chili pepper

mallet

slice of
pizza

ruler

pennant

doughnut

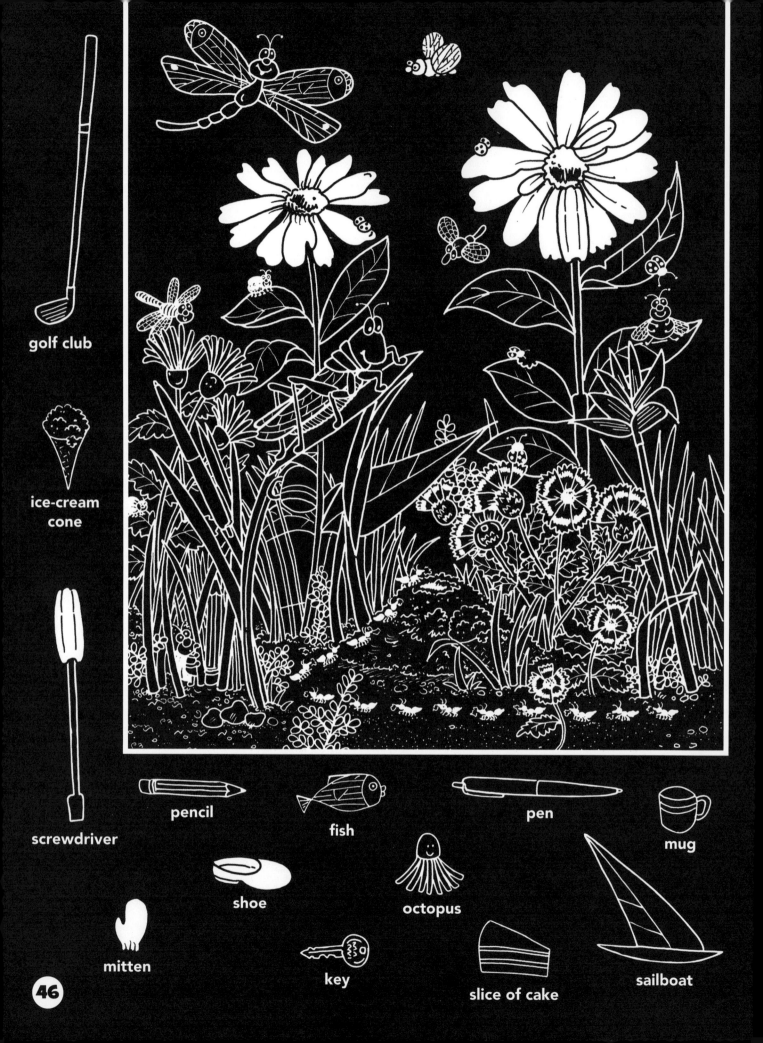

golf club

ice-cream cone

screwdriver

pencil

fish

pen

mug

shoe

octopus

mitten

key

slice of cake

sailboat

baseball bat

bottle

pennant

needle

party hat

shoe

drinking cup

clothespin

open book

toothbrush

pencil

carrot

mushroom

47

GRAB A BARREL

book

baseball
cap

tube of
toothpaste

horseshoe

banana

slice of pizza

toothbrush

artist's brush

scrub brush

boot

teacup

megaphone

saucepan

mallet

candle

sock

cupcake

flashlight

bell

slice of pizza

wrench

vase

slice of pizza

pine tree

bat

heart

angelfish

bird

artist's brush

wedge of lemon

pen

canoe

needle

banana

slice of pizza

crown

slice of pie

ice-cream bar

baseball

heart

ruler

teacup

tennis racket

banana

bowling pin

pickle

sailboat

crescent moon

wedge of lemon

shoe

flag

magnet

candle

taco shell

crown

slice of pie

crescent moon

ice-cream bar

seashell

butter knife

tack

spoon

heart

magic wand

54

bell

candle

glove

flashlight

artist's brush

toothbrush

briefcase

pennant

ruler

wristwatch

saw

boot

crown

skateboard

yo-yo

slice of
bread

pencil

banana

tack

feather

bell

frying pan

apple

golf club

pennant

boomerang

comb

crescent
moon

magnet

bow tie

golf club

drinking
straw

candy corn

wedge of
lemon

heart

ruler

seashell

tooth

glove

sock

shovel

test tube

toothbrush

pencil

party
hat

puzzle piece

58

ring

ice-cream cone

paper clip

banana

crown

toothbrush

bow tie

shoe

book

glove

hat

sailboat

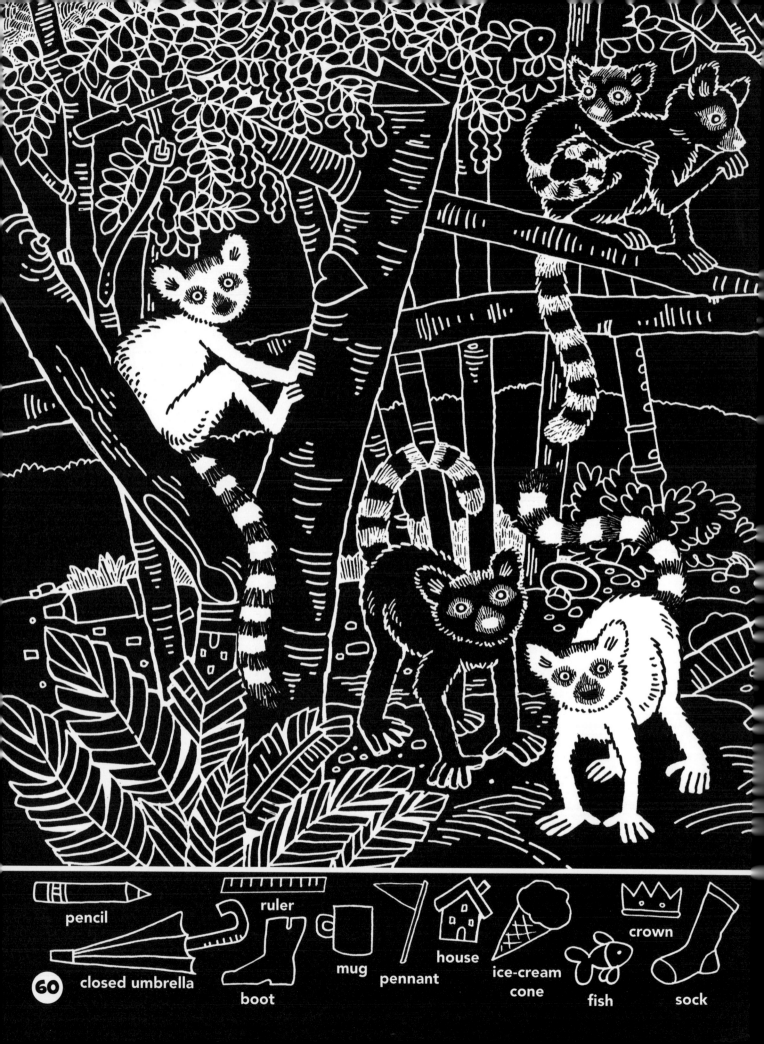

pencil

ruler

closed umbrella

boot

mug

pennant

house

ice-cream cone

crown

fish

sock

cupcake   sheep   comb   heart   toothbrush
spool of thread   trowel   tube of toothpaste

recorder   crayon   belt   ring   spoon   screwdriver

adhesive bandage

spool of thread

pencil

candle

wedge of lemon

waffle

kite

fishhook

fish

turtle

baseball glove

ice-cream cone

birthday cake

comb

snowman

sailboat

slice of pie

paintbrush

ruler

slice of watermelon

pen

ship

magnifying glass

needle

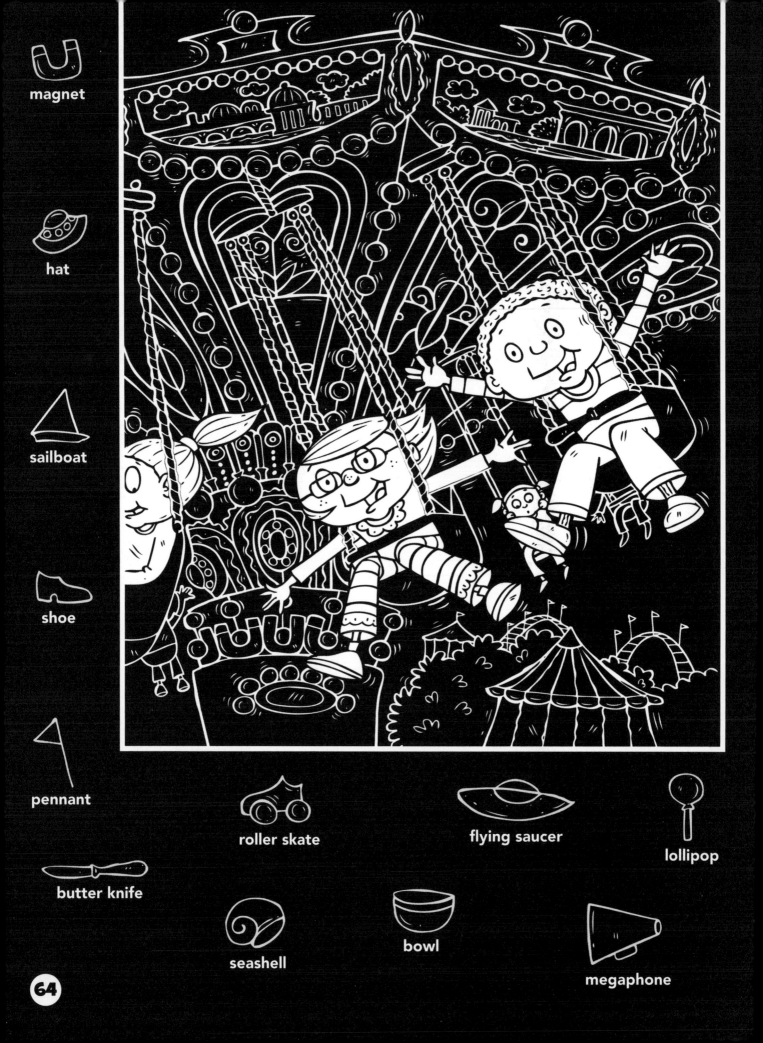

magnet

hat

sailboat

shoe

pennant

roller skate

flying saucer

lollipop

butter knife

seashell

bowl

megaphone

64

mushroom

slice of bread

saltshaker

teacup

heart

handbell

open book

toothbrush

artist's brush

pitcher

button

glove

doughnut

fish

feather

boot

chef's hat

envelope

dog bone

artist's brush

balloon

button

teacup

ghost

ice-cream cone

lollipop

banana

67

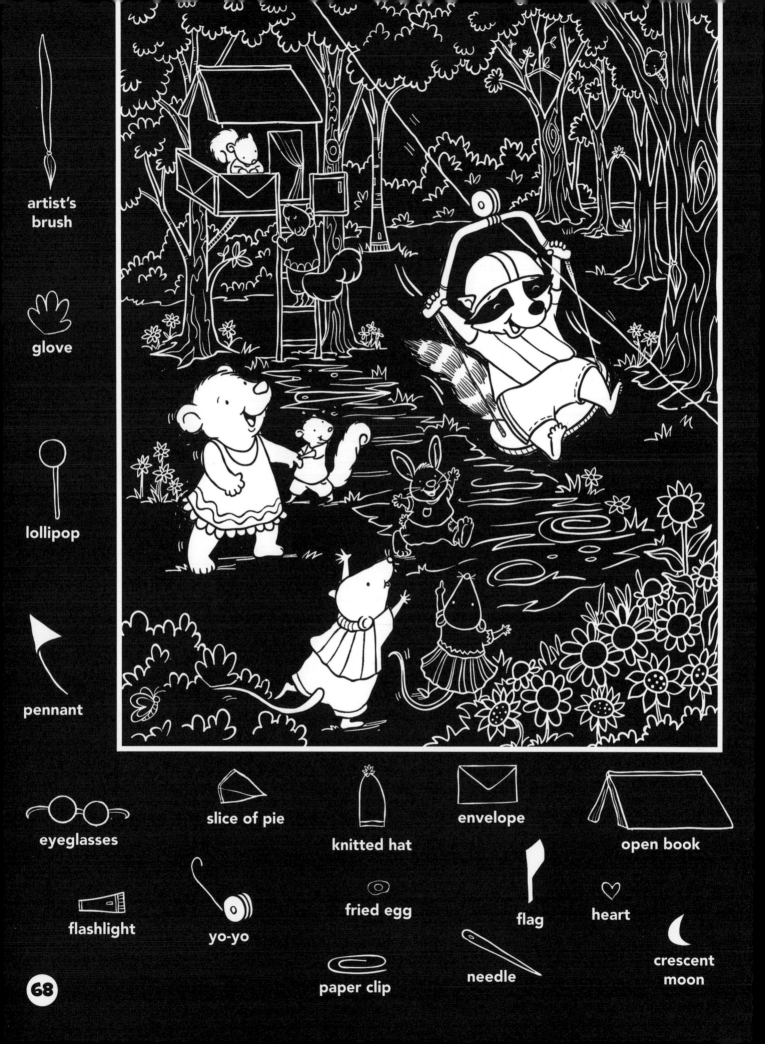

artist's brush

glove

lollipop

pennant

eyeglasses

slice of pie

knitted hat

envelope

open book

flashlight

yo-yo

fried egg

flag

heart

needle

paper clip

crescent moon

68

pencil

heart

handbell

coat hanger

paper clip

banana

carrot

egg

hammer

fish

horn

sailboat

bird

nail

tooth

olive

piece of popcorn

candy corn

cinnamon bun

cookie

boomerang

paper airplane

crown

mitten

bell

needle

ruler

sailboat

shuttlecock

fish

banana

heart

drumstick

boot

mushroom

comb

glove

celery

carrot

mushroom

banana

crescent
moon

comb

fan

button

tube of
toothpaste

wedge of
lemon

lock

candle

ice pop

slice of
pie

bat

vase

turtle

fried egg

71

toothbrush

cane

book

paintbrush

ice-cream
cone

paper clip

slice of pizza

crescent moon

hoe

hat

crayon

saltshaker

fried egg

ring

baseball bat

tennis racket

mitten

seashell

ladder

spool of thread

lemon   horseshoe   glove   sock   ice-cream cone   feather   slice of cake   canoe

paintbrush   fish   banana

75

banana

pencil

mushroom

feather

T-shirt

heart

bird

fish

paper clip

bell

eyeglasses

glove

spoon

ring

crown

ice-cream cone

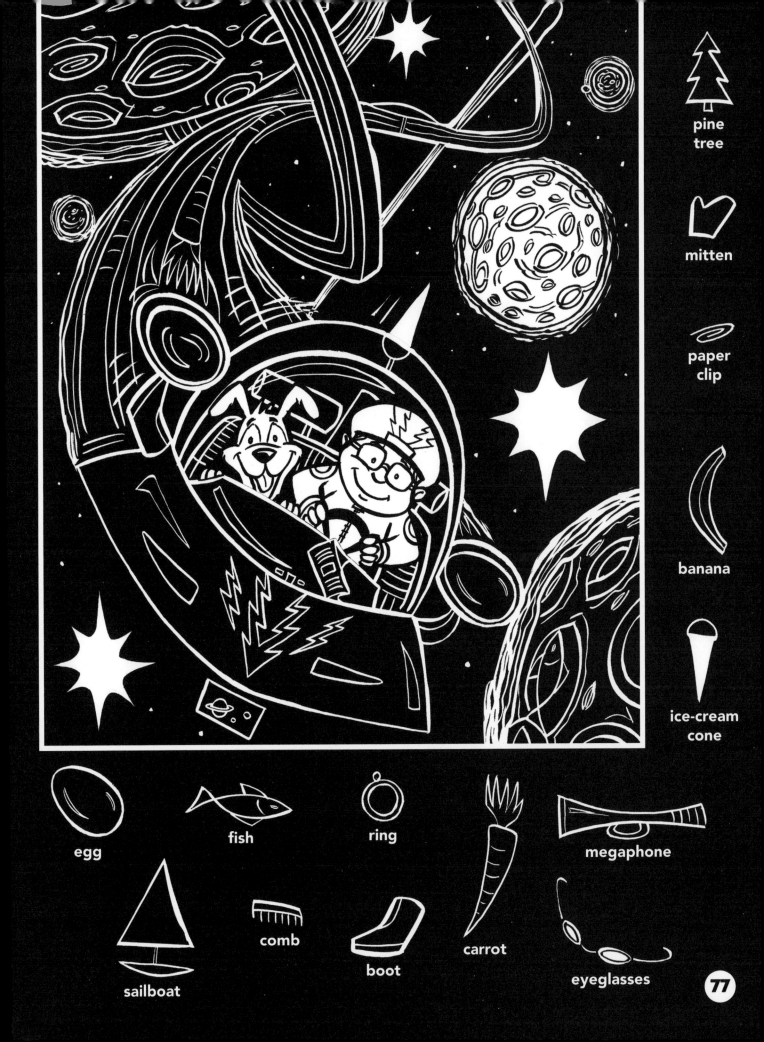

pine
tree

mitten

paper
clip

banana

ice-cream
cone

egg

fish

ring

megaphone

sailboat

comb

boot

carrot

eyeglasses

77

bird

ice-cream bar

party hat

pear

slice of pizza

fish

envelope

ruler

hammer

pencil

knitted hat

purse

79

dog bone

seashell

feather

diamond

fishhook

wedge of lemon

comb

teardrop

birdhouse

eraser

envelope

snow cone

snow
cone

crescent
moon

handbell

star

high-heeled shoe

heart

crown

hat

paper clip

toothbrush

glove

banana

bird

tea bag

spatula

ice-cream bar

ladder

flag

ring

open book

spoon

needle

domino

mallet

funnel

heart

top hat

toothbrush

horseshoe

envelope

sailboat

mushroom

lollipop

spool of thread

tack

bowl

slice of pie

83

comb

spoon

pencil

bow tie

mitten

ladle

drumstick

crayon

drinking straw

paper clip

ice-cream cone

broccoli

84

mug

toothbrush

envelope

crown

slice of pie

ruler

yo-yo

skateboard

snake

carrot

strawberry

seashell

heart

cookie

spoon

mitten

magic wand

crown

ruler

coat hanger

crescent moon

lightning bolt

hockey stick

wishbone

ice-cream bar

chili pepper

fish

teacup

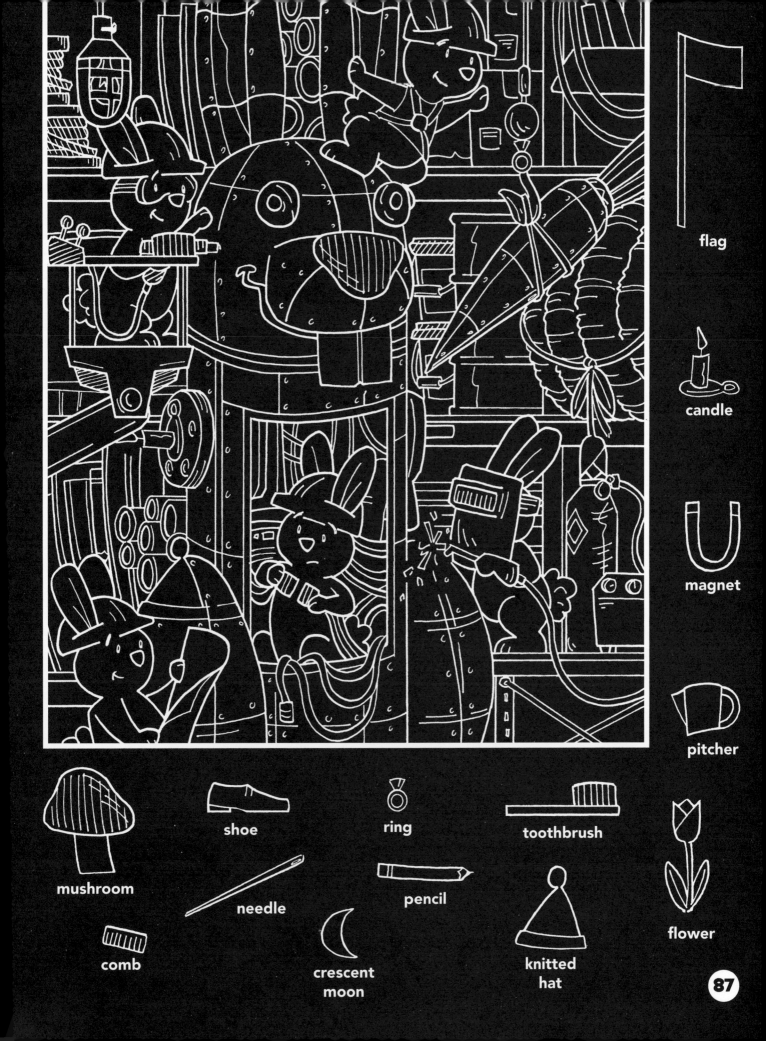

flag

candle

magnet

pitcher

mushroom

shoe

ring

toothbrush

flower

needle

pencil

comb

crescent
moon

knitted
hat

87

Pages 2–3

Page 4

Page 5

Pages 6–7

Page 8

Page 9

Page 10

Page 11

Pages 12–13

Page 14

Page 15

Page 16

Page 17

Page 18

Page 19

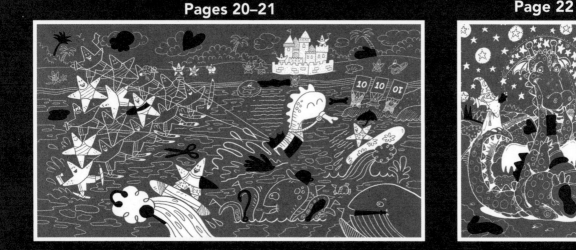

Page 29

Pages 30–31

Page 32

Page 33

Page 34

Page 35

Page 36

Page 37

Pages 38–39

Page 40

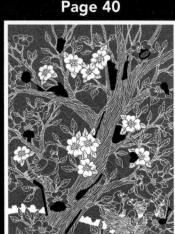

Page 41

Pages 42–43

Pages 44–45

Page 46

Answers

Page 47

Pages 48–49

Pages 50–51

Page 52

Page 53

Page 54

Page 55

Answers

Pages 56–57

Page 58

Page 59

Pages 60–61

Pages 62–63

Page 64

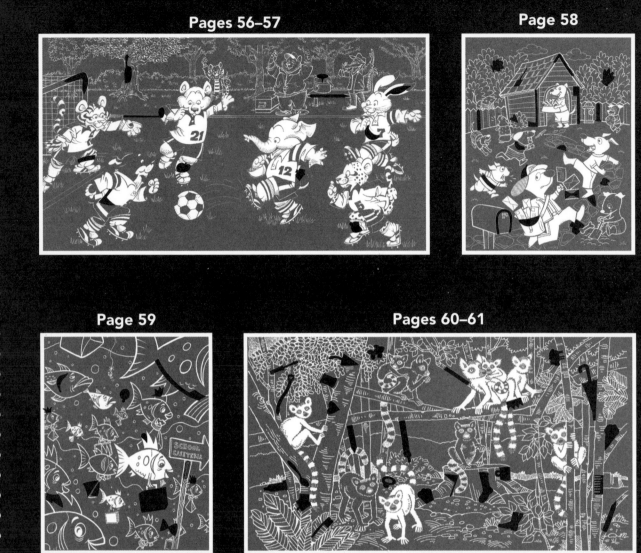

Answers

Page 65

Pages 66–67

Page 68

Page 69

Page 70

Page 71

Pages 72–73

Answers

Pages 74–75

Page 76

Page 77

Pages 78–79

Pages 80–81

Page 82